T5-AGA-561

.The Personality Factor

Jason Leigh

 AIRBORNE PRESS San Francisco, California

THE PERSONALITY FACTOR

Published by:

Airborne Press
Presidio 29355
San Francisco, CA 94129, U. S. A.

All rights reserved. The desires of the author that the concept of the **Personality Factor** be as widely disseminated as possible supercedes his interest in monetary gain. The publishers accede to his request: this material may be freely reproduced for students or other educational endeavors and for training and research purposes. There is no requirement to obtain special permission. However, the material cannot be sold in any form to include the systematic or large scale reproduction as inclusion in items for sale is strictly prohibited.

Copyright @ 1986 by Airborne Press
Printed in the United States of America

BF
698,4
.L45
1986

Library of Congress Cataloging in Publication Data.
Leigh, Jason
    The Personality Factor
Biography: p.
Includes index.
1. Typology (Psychology)
2. Myers-Briggs Type Indicator.
3. Psychology, Applied.
l. Title.
BF698.4.L45 1985 155.2'64 85-26689
ISBN 0-934145-22-6 Softcover

WARNING !

This book is designed to discuss the author's view of the **Personality Factor**. He does not claim to have the last word. There are hundreds of personality instruments available to the general public. The author's desire is not to add to those. His insertion of the **Job Stick**, designed by him is intended just for the use of this book and to make the concept of the **Personality Factor** meaningful. It is not the purpose of the author or publisher to exhaust all the information available on the subject. Many references are available to the reader, many of which are listed in the back of the book. The purpose of this book is to educate and set forth the author's belief that the quality of life for the reader can be greatly enhanced through the book's reading. However, the author and Airborne Press shall have neither liability nor responsibility to any person or entity with respect to any loss or damage caused or alleged caused directly or indirectly by the information contained in this book.

If you do not agree with the above, you may return this book to the publisher for a full refund.

References

Autry, J. (1975) *Unpublished Paper*, Ball State University, Muncie, IN.

de Laszto, V. (Ed) (1959) *The Basic Writings of C.G. Jung*, New York: Modern Library, Random House.

Hall, C., Nordly V. (Ed) (1973) *A Primer of Jungian Psychology*, New York: Mentor.

Keirsey-Bates (1978) *Please Understand Me*, Del Mar, CA: Prometheus Nemesis Books.

Jung, C. (1923) *Psychological Types*, New York: Harcourt Brace.

Myers, I. (1962) *Manual: The Myers-Briggs Type Indicator*, Palo Alto, California,: Consulting Psychologists Press.

Powell, J. (1976) *Fully Human, Fully Alive*, Niles, Illinois: Argus Communications.

Tournier, P. (1954) *A Doctor's Casebook*, London: SCM Press.

Wheelwright, J. (1964) *Manuel for Jungian Type Survey* (Gray-Wheelwright Test, 16th Revision). Palo Alto: Society of Jungian Analysts of Northern California.

PREFACE

"I am neither spurred on by excessive optimism nor in love with high ideals, but am merely concerned with the fate of the individual human being - that infinitesimal unit on whom a world depends, and in whom, if we read the meaning of the Christian message right, even God seeks his goal."

- Carl Jung

"But, Mr. Johnson, I can't do a thing with him at home."

"Have you thought about putting him somewhere?"

"Oh no, I don't mean he's mean, just doesn't seem like other children his age."

The above conversation took place between my mother and the elementary school principal when I was in fifth grade. I still remember being frightened. A ten-year-old boy scared out of his wits about going to reform school. Why? Is he beating up little old ladies, mugging people on the subway, swearing obscenities?

No. Mainly, he's being a ten-year-old. Different from his classmates. A shorter attention span in school, laughing out loud, making girls cry, staring out the window, forgetting homework, not remembering books.

Fortunately for me, my mother didn't take the school principal too seriously. She did, however, recognize that I was different, but figured I'd grow out of it. Plus, she shrugged, wasn't I like my father, anyway? After all, he was different and drove her continuously to distraction. Her usual line was that she had never thought about divorcing Dad but killing him often. In addition to working a steady job, he had ten other things on the side.

The man invented embarrassment. When friends came calling, he would soon be bored with the chitchat and go to bed, but usually say, "if you'd go home, we'd go to bed," laughing all the way.

I could easily write a dozen books about my father. To others he seemed weird and out of touch, but to me he was Jonathan Livingston Seagull, and could be his "own best friend," or "OK," long before anybody had to tell him. I know now that Dad was not a weirdo, but out of "sync" with most, and definitely a "different drummer" type. But, he was OK; and **it's OK to be different.**

ALL ARE DIFFERENT

In over twenty five years of practicing my profession, I have worked with thousands of people and am still constantly awed by their individual differences. The fact that we are born differently is logical and natural and yet the concept seems to have eluded most of the experts. The one exception being Carl Jung, the Swiss born psychiatrist, who concluded that the inescapable truth is that the personality differences in mankind have some sort of biological foundation. We are born with a particular personality orientation. (Jung, 1921)

People's personalities dictate their actions. This is called the **Personality Factor.** An example: one Christmas, I was in a busy department store. People were bustling, hustling, fretting, pushing, shoving. Tempers were on edge and for the most part, the holiday spirit was not to be found.

Into this atmosphere came one of those rare persons, seemingly oblivious to the world which most of us inhabit, laughing, talking to strangers, and ignoring all but his own existence. To the lady at the perfume counter he said, "My you smell good." She laughs, as he looks at an overweight, fiftyish woman peering from behind large framed glasses. "Now sweetie, you dab a little of this "Charlie" behind your ear, and you'll turn on half this store."

What enables this character to be uninhibited? Crazy? Maybe, but more than likely just **different.** Have you ever seen anyone walk into a crowded elevator and start talking to strangers? Or get on the N train at Times Square, heading downtown (Brooklyn), and call out the stops like a conductor: "fifty-ninth Street, watch your step!"

Have you ever wondered how a guy like McMurphy, in One Flew Over The Cuckoo's Nest could be so freed up? Or why Nixon did not burn the Watergate tapes? Ever think about why Janis Joplin killed herself, or Elvis Presley could not live with his success? I can tell you one thing they all had in common: their personalities. The individual differences and the drive that gave them their uniqueness: the collective part of their being we call the **Personality Factor** contributed both to their success and most likely to their demise.

Chapter I

THE PERSONALITY FACTOR IS YOU

In this chapter, you will discover in capsule form the theory of the **Personality Factor** and how it can be measured. After digesting the information, you will begin to have an understanding of:

☥   Why a definition of the personality is so hard to come by.

☥   The subtle but distinctive Jungian view of personality.

☥   The enormous contributions of Katherine Briggs and Isabel Myers in determining the **Personality Factor.**

THE PERSONALITY FACTOR

Your personality is what you are! Why is such a truth so hard to grasp? Libraries are filled with books about personality, and entire college courses are devoted to "theories of personality." However, most deal with individual differences and the maturation process with little or no reference to how personality is lived out in everyday life. This is the **Personality Factor** and is crucial to your well being.

Traditionally, personality has been equated with social adroitness. We see someone as having a "good" or "a lot of personality," and the term has many definitions, with no single meaning universally accepted.   Modern psychology has offered little remedy and, for the most part, has been confusing. From the beginning, the fathers of psychology have made a practice of cancelling out each other's theories.

The individual personality differences of Freud, Jung, Reich, Horney, Erickson, Fromm, Maslow, Ellis, and Rogers, to name a few, are expressions of the very problem. Consequently, there are as many theories as theoreticians.   Words such as temperament, nature, disposition, character, and individual differences get confused through semantics and lose their usefulness.

HIPPOCRATES

The idea of the **Personality Factor** is not new. Hippocrates, the brilliant Greek physician and philosopher, identified four basic types of personality. He gave them names based on body liquids: *sanguine, choleric, melancholy,* and *phlegmatic.* The notion that body liquids determined personality has long since been discarded, but surprisingly, his personality classification has remained.

Noted Swiss psychiatrist Carl Jung, building on Hippocrates' idea, first presented his views in Psychological Types in Zurich in 1921. They centered around the idea that personality is not random or haphazard, but actually does have an observable pattern. Put another way, personality determines behavior.

Simply, personality is what we are. Personality is one's personal signature, the individual differences by which we are known. The way we act, react, make decisions, view the world, and live out our lives are the graphics of these differences. This is the **Personality Factor.**

MODERN DAY PSYCHOLOGICAL PIONEERS

Jung's work in psychological types would probably have languished in obscurity had it not been for a mother and daughter team, Katherine and Isabel Briggs-Myers. Together, they painstakingly, with very little encouragement from any direction and, in fact, disdain from the academic and psychology community, developed an easy-to-use questionnaire of 166 short questions and word-pair combinations called the Myers Briggs Type Indicator (MBTI). Until the MBTI came along, there was no real way to measure the **Personality Factor.**

A REMARKABLE WOMAN

Katherine Briggs, a quiet observer of mankind, became fascinated with individual differences. Quite on her own, she observed and collected data which she began to formulate into a "personality typing" theory. She discovered Jung's typology views, adopted them, and began to use his general framework to expand on the likenesses and differences she saw inherent in us all.

From that beginning, Katherine and later her daughter, Isabel, succeeded in developing the MBTI, which from her initial fascination with likenesses and differences in people has become the most widely used personality instrument for normal (noninstitutionalized) populations in America.

It is a simple instrument where a person selects between responses, based on natural choices such as "Does a schedule (a) appeal to you (b) cramp you?" (Myers, 1976)

HOW RATHER THAN WHY PERSONALITY DIFFERS

The mother and daughter team and their development of the <u>Type</u> <u>Indicator</u> picked up on a basic difference in Jung and Freud. Jung was not so much interested in the causative sources of personality as in the behavior of the individual. It is the individual's behavior that is the foundation of the <u>Myers Briggs Type Indicator</u>. Simply stated, the <u>Indicator</u> measures personality differences.(Myers, 1976)

In my thinking, these two incredible females, Katherine Briggs and daughter, Isabel, with this instrument have revolutionized the entire field of psychology. The **Personality Factor** is the result of taking the conceptual framework of Jung's typology, measuring it through the <u>MBTI</u> and seeing yourself as the unique human being you are.

CHAPTER II

This above all, to thine own self be true, and it must follow as the night, the day, thou canst then be false to any man.

- **Shakespeare**

JOB STICK

This chapter focuses on giving you handles on your **Personality Factor.** Five Years ago, I designed, tested, redesigned, tested adinfinitum a self scoring instrument I've called **The Job Stick.** In no way is it considered a valid instrument. I've used it in scores of seminars, conferences, and with clients when time was limited. Always I've said; "If we had time, you should take the <u>Meyers Briggs Type Indicator.</u>

I designed the **Job Stick** to merely show and demonstrate the individual **Personality Factor.** Under no circumstances is it to be considered a substitute for the <u>MBTI.</u> This book could not be meaningful without understanding how you arrive at the **Personality Factor.** In this chapter you will:

✿ Take and self score the **Job Stick.**Understand that only you can decide what the **PF** is in your life.

✿ Become familiar with the language of the **PF**

✿ Memorize your **PF** letters and have a general understanding of the meaning.

Instructions: the following phrases are pairs (a&b), make a check in front of the phrase you like best; You may not like either one, but to understand the PF (personality factor), choose one.

I LIKE:

☐ 1a to find out what others are thinking before making a decision.
☐ 1b to do my own thing.

☐ 2a being called an imaginative worker.
☐ 2b to work with facts.

☐ 3a to analyze a situation.
☐ 3b to go with my feelings.

☐ 4a to let people do their own thing.
☐ 4b to influence people toward my way of thinking.

☐ 5a to have space.
☐ 5b to be with people most of the time.

☐ 6a using trusted methods to get the job done.
☐ 6b to figure out a better way to do things.

☐ 7a making decisions based on fact.
☐ 7b to decide what the impact will be upon people.

☐ 8a to avoid exact schedules.
☐ 8b to stick to deadlines.

☐ 9a briefly discussing a subject and then thinking to myself about it.
☐ 9b talking for a long time about a subject and thinking about it at a later time.

☐ 10a thinking about what could be.
☐ 10b looking at what is.

☐ 11a to think.
☐ 11b to feel.

☐ 12a making quick decisions so I can move on.
☐ 12b to carefully consider an issue and then make a firm decision.

☐ 13a to hold things close to my chest.
☐ 13b sharing activities with others.

☐ 14a to philosophize.
☐ 14b the real and actual.

☐ 15a helping others.
☐ 15b letting people decide for themselves.

☐ 16a to look at my options.
☐ 16b being prepared in advance.

☐ 17a to think of myself as open and friendly with everybody.
☐ 17b to have depth relationships with a few people.

☐ 18a taking risks if there is a possibility of succeeding.
☐ 18b to play it safe and go with the known.

☐ 19a to go with what seems right.
☐ 19b to analyze, to reason, look at the facts in making a   decision.

☐ 20a to plan ahead.
☐ 20b to go with the flow.

☐ 21a to meet new people.
☐ 21b being alone with old friends.

☐ 22a ideas.
☐ 22b objective data.

☐ 23a to go with my values.
☐ 23b measurable results.

☐ 24a being organized.
☐ 24b spontaneity.

☐ 25a discussing issued extensively with friends.
☐ 25b thinking over an issue in my mind.

☐ 26a the well-laid out executed plan.
☐ 26b to have a plan just in case.

☐ 27a logical people.
☐ 27b gutsy people.

☐ 28a freedom to change my mind.
☐ 28b plans locked in concrete.

☐ 29a attracting attention.
☐ 29b going unnoticed.

☐ 30a looking ahead at the future.
☐ 30b the here and now.

- ☐ 31a excitement.
- ☐ 31b calmness.

- ☐ 32a being on time.
- ☐ 32b letting it happen.

- ☐ 33a introducing others to strangers.
- ☐ 33b being introduced.

- ☐ 34a to keep my checkbook balanced to the penny.
- ☐ 34b my checkbook to be accurate within a few cents.

- ☐ 35a to think I am sensitive to people and situations.
- ☐ 35b to think I am realistic about life.

- ☐ 36a organization, planning, orderliness.
- ☐ 36b flexibility, minimum planning, happenings.

INSTRUCTIONS: Transfer your check marks from the boxes beside your choice to the appropriate blanks below. Be careful to put the checks in the proper spaces. Total the amount of checks under each letter and put that number at the bottom.

<u>E</u>	<u>I</u>	<u>S</u>	<u>N</u>
1a.____	1b.____	2b.____	2a.____
5b.____	5a.____	6a.____	6b.____
9b.____	9a.____	10b.____	10a.____
13b.____	13a.____	14b.____	14a.____
17b.____	17a.____	18b.____	18a.____
21a.____	21b.____	22b.____	22b.____
25a.____	25b.____	26b.____	26a.____
29a.____	29b.____	30b.____	30a.____
33a.____	33b.____	34a.____	34b.____

TOTALS: E   I   S   N

____   ____   ____   ____

T	F	J	P
3a.____	3b.____	4b.____	4a.____
7a.____	7b.____	8b.____	8a.____
11a.____	11b.____	12b.____	12a.____
15b.____	15a.____	16b.____	16a.____
19b.____	19a.____	20a.____	20b.____
23b.____	23a.____	24a.____	24b.____
27a.____	27b.____	28b.____	28a.____
31b.____	31a.____	32a.____	32b.____
35b.____	35a____	36a.____	36b.____

TOTALS: T   F   J   P

____   ____   ____   ____

Transfer the highest score for your E-I, S-N, T-F, and J-P lines. If your E is higher than I, you are an E, put the E on the line below. Do the same with the others.

____ ____ ____ ____

This is your **Personality Factor.**

Chapter III

YOUR TYPING TABLE

Take a look at the combinations that make up your personality. Look at yours and see how well it fits. If it doesn't, find one that does. These are merely capsules developed over a long period of time and with thousands of people. They certainly are not all inclusive, but every word and phrase has been excrusiatingly scrutinized. They can be extremely useful in helping see the big picture of the **Personality Factor.** Also, they are prescriptive. I'm not into sitting back with no definite views on how the **PF** can help you in your life.

Prescriptive

All of the "capsules" are prescriptive: meaning they describe what all the factors add up to in making a whole. Then, they say some things to possibly consider in dealing with areas of life that may be unproductive.

I once gave the "typing table" to a thousand people. It was in the course of an after dinner speech. An unbelievable miscue in tactics. The audience was gone forever. My purpose had been to illustrate the tremendous significance of the **Personality Factor.** Once they recognized themselves in the short profiles, I could not finish because of the questions.

JUDGING (J)

	EXTROVERT (E)	**INTROVERT (I)**
Sensing Thinking (ST)	ESTJ NAME:_____ A good business person, you can organize and produce desired results. Practical. Love structure. Rules. Procedures. Do well with bureaucracy. Desire to have control. Often accused of being unromantic. Try giving yourself some freedom through meaningful relationships and activites. Experience a few different way of doing things.	ISTJ NAME:_____ You are the organizational person: thorough, down-to-earth and traditional. Dependable. Can sit at a desk or computer terminal for hours. Not easily distracted. Can be highly critical. Myopic. Stubborn. Your view is not always right or best. Work at being more impartial. Serious. Try doing some things just for fun.
Sensing Feeling (SF)	ESFJ NAME:_____ Sociable and likeable, you love being around your friends and work to make all have a good experience. Good conversationalist. Thoughtful. People matter more than principles. Desire to be affirmed. Can have low tolerance for stress, resulting in poorly thought out decisions. Because of your high need to please people, be objective in relationships.	ISFJ NAME:_____ Quietly serve mankind. Your responsible nature exemplifies honesty and principled behavior. Detailed and accurate. Willing to stay with the job until completed. Can become preoccupied to the exclusion of all else or others. Close friends often misunderstand. Be aware. Sometimes intolerant. Try giving credit to others whose ideas differ from yours.
Intuitive Thinking (NT)	ENTJ NAME:_____ A good manager, you can run any organization, and well. Intelligent. Confident. Purposeful. Radiate confidence which sometimes threatens people. May make snap judgments with wrong conclusions. Use your analytical and rational side to avoid such difficulties. "Workaholic" attitude. Give yourself license for more leisure activities and less work.	INTJ NAME:_____ The great thinker. Your ideas are often novel, occasionally offbeat, unusual, and original. Organized. Independent. Determined. Sometimes suspicious and cynical. Don't automatically distrust people's motives until you have reason. Try to see all sides of an argument. Can be obstinate and outwardly unemotional. Relax and pay some quality attention to others.
Intuitive Feeling (NF)	ENFJ NAME:_____ Adept at handling people, you have a talent for cutting right to the heart of any matter. Responsible. Concerned. Care about other's feelings. Well liked. Hospitable. Accessible. May on occasion over-identify with people and situations. Can give chameleon effect. Quit trying to be all things to all people.	INFJ NAME:_____ Tenacious. A good worker, you can be counted upon to do your share and more. Persistent. Creative. Personable. Perfectionist. Be careful, lest you put an inordinate amount of time and energy into something with little payoff. Desire harmony, but can result in a loss of orginal purpose. Wake up to realism; the world will not always like or agree with you. Don't get down.

PERCEPTIVE (P)

EXTROVERT (E)　　　　　　INTROVERT (I)

ESTP

NAME:_____

Spontaneity is the driving force in your life. Master of the grand gesture. Good entrepreneur. Don't mind taking a risk. Occasionally appear blunt and indifferent. Non-traditional. Don't let your bent on doing things differently rule out what presently works. Friends are not objects and therefore, expendable. Develop some in-depth relationships.

ISTP

NAME:_____

Laid back, composed, you look at life swirling around you with candid amazement. Why and how are key words. Good with mechanics or tools. A craftsperson. Your desire for expediency is often called lackadaisical by critics. Emotionally invest yourself in something. Sometimes distant. For your own good, don't neglect social contacts.

Sensing Thinking (ST)

ESFP

NAME:_____

The life of the party. You are gregarious and fun to be around. Positive. Sports minded. Skillful with groups of people. The entertainer. Make sure your need to be on center stage doesn't turn off your fans. You live for the NOW to the exclusion of anything else. Decide what your future is five years from now and how you're to get there.

ISFP

NAME:_____

Modest. Live and let live is a personal creed. Relaxed and at ease. Kind and considerate. Love nature. You avoid arguments which makes you an easy target for aggressive and uncaring people. Sometimes accused of living in a world all your own. Be cautious to the impulses that might lead you to abandon present responsibilities for some illusive dream.

Sensing Feeling (SF)

ENTP

NAME:_____

Many interests. Alert. Resourceful. Never dull. Can't stand to be bored. A bit of the crusader. You can't fight every battle. Pick and choose carefully. Sometimes thought to be insensitive. Usually just zoned out, but people can't be expected to know. Be aware of feelings, especially the "significant others" in your life.

INTP

NAME:_____

Objective. Logical. Smart. Can excel in those areas that interest you. A great idea person, not big on follow-up. Mostly shun the limelight which results in accusations of aloofness. Some truth as you choose to spend a great deal of time alone. Try a little social activity, even when you don't think you're in the mood and see how it fits.

Intuitive Thinking (NT)

ENFP

NAME:_____

Lively. Vivacious. Enthusiastic. A problem solver, you leap to the aid of friends. Generous. See the big picture without worrying about details. Quick to form subjective opinions. May have trigger temper. Try the old count to ten trick when something angers you. Occasionally rationalize for convenience. Develop a life strategy and be cautious with projects and personal commitments.

INFP

NAME:_____

Your creativity and innovative nature combine to accomplish much. Hearty. Loyal. Involved in numerous activities, often too many. Concentrate your efforts on a few projects and avoid the cliche "jack of all trades, master of none." Friendly, but often so reserved that people don't realize it. Increase social activities, especially with good friends.

Intuitive Feeling (NF)

CHAPTER IV

BORN TO BE DIFFERENT

In this chapter, the emphasis is on:

✤ The importance of knowing <u>your</u> individual **Personality Type**

✤ Understanding the different factors making up <u>your</u> **Personality Type.**

MOVED TO ACTION

I've been down the psychological trail for years, and have chased every elusive "rabbit track" in existence. Some have been enlightening, some painful, others insightful. From Esalen's encounter groups to primal scream therapy, I've been there. I've studied scripting, Gestalt, psycho-drama, and after twenty five years and thousands of dollars, not to mention time, understanding the significance of my individual differences and that they made up my **Personality Factor** did more than everything else put together. The <u>Myers Briggs Type Indicator</u> measured this **Personality Type** for me. The feedback was like looking into my soul. All my life, even as a youngster, I had this feeling that I was a little crazy. I didn't think like other people, looked at most pronouncements with skepticism and never seemed to fit comfortably into the usual molds.

Understanding my **Personality Factor** makes me

realize that I, like my dad, listened to the beat of a "different drummer." As an ENTP, my natural choices often put me out of "sync" with others. My "intuitive" nature kept me from concentrating on one idea because it created ten others. I was always looking for more and more information. People called me indecisive. To think they were right, infuriated me. Accepting my individual dfferences started me doing something about it. The difference is that people could tell me forever; however, seeing it in black and white moved me to action.

Now, take a look at the individual portions that go to make up the whole of your PF. The different letters that represent your **Personality Factor** have special meaning to you. They are you! Although the language is new and the terminology is looked upon by many people as a cross between alphabet soup and birth signs, memorizing and getting the letters firmly fixed in your mind cannot be overemphasized.

Over the years as I've tested thousands of people, I often ask them, "what is your profile or **Personality Factor.**" Most can't remember. Remembering is the first step in allowing the **PF** to have some real impact in your life.

E - EXTROVERTS   I - INTROVERTS

Extroverts are energized toward people and the outside world. They are charged up by being around people and events.

Introverts are independent, quiet, and don't mind working alone. Usually socially reserved.

S - SENSORS   N - INTUITIVES

Sensor's choices revolve around the concrete and the actual. They are detailed; zero in on what is, the structured, the rules.

iNtuitives are possibility and project oriented. The big picture is in focus but the nitty gritty escapes them.

T - THINKERS   F - FEELERS

Thinkers look at life in terms of logic, what-ifs and objectivity. Decisions are made in terms of the Pros and Cons.

Feelers are empathetic, sensitive, and consider personal values as part of the process; desire harmony and like to get along.

J - JUDGERS   P - PERCEIVERS

The **Judger** is decisive, firm, a decision maker; knows what must be done and does it; comes to closure; sets goals; is achievement-oriented.

The **Perceiver** is open-ended, flexible. Going from point A to point B; gets a better offer; takes it; rolls with the punches.

ONLY YOU CAN DETERMINE YOUR PERSONALITY

One of the most difficult parts of dealing with any psychometric instrument is placing too much importance upon it. When I use the **Personality Factor** as a distinct counseling technique , I say, "does this make sense to you, does this profile fit you." Or, if it doesn't, "do you see one that does." **Only you can decide.**

However, having said the above , you say , "Yes, it fits or most of it fits," then I say, "What equally is important is what it doesn't say. *Jung said that with every positive side, there is always a negative.* Shown below are the positives and the negatives of the individual **Factors**.

PLUSES AND MINUSES OF YOUR PERSONALITY

PLUSES   MINUSES

Extroverts

PLUSES	MINUSES
people oriented	little reflection time
active	talks too much
positive	often impatient

Sensor

PLUSES	MINUSES
detail oriented	misses big picture
practical	little imagination
trusts the senses	mistrusts the new

Thinker

PLUSES	MINUSES
analytical	misses the obvious
sees all sides	can be unfeeling
fair minded	sometimes uncompromising

Judger

PLUSES	MINUSES
makes decisions	often inflexible
likes control	critical
comes to closure	always task oriented

PLUSES   MINUSES

Introverts

PLUSES	MINUSES
can work alone	often secretive
stictuitiveness	slow to act
strong convictions	often withdrawn

iNtuitive

PLUSES	MINUSES
imagines possibilities	too future oriented
problem solver	forgets details
unafraid of complicated	impulsive

Feeler

PLUSES	MINUSES
Loves touching	sometimes naive
sensitive	emotional reactions
value oriented	spur of the moment

Perceiver

PLUSES	MINUSES
open ended	indecisive
flexible	changes mind
gathers information	unfinished projects

CHAPTER V

ARE YOU AN INTROVERT(I)
OR
EXTROVERT(E)

YOU DECIDE

Y ou will:

 Recognize **introversion**(I) and **extroversion**(E) as an attitude.

 See the characteristics of each.

 Become more comfortable with your orientation toward being an **introvert**(I) or an **extrovert**(E).

Introversion(I) and Extroversion(E)

There is an attitude very distinctive in **introversion**(I) and **extroversion**(E). Jung calls it "an attitude to an object." I see it more in observation and description. For instance, if the degree of **extroversion**(E) or **introversion**(I) is high, you will have no doubt. The high extrovert can't be quiet and is definitely uncomfortable with silence. The high **introvert**(I) is quite the opposite. He/she revels in silence and solitude.

I still remember an embarrassing time. Serving as the escort to a somewhat well known person who had come as a featured "expert" speaker, I was anxious to be at my most clever self **extroverted**(E) self. Finally, the "expert" said to me, "Would you please be quiet?"

Introversion(I) and **extroversion**(E) are Jungian terms but not pitted one against the other. One simply **is**

an **introvert**(I)   or   extrovert(E).   **Extroverts**(E)
appear to be more common and unfortunately often touted
as "better" because of good people skills: backslapping,
gregarious while those more reticent, quiet, or thoughtful
somehow are thought to be "not quite to be up to par."
Nothing could be further from the truth.

As   a   **Personality   Factor,   introverts**(I)   and
extroverts(E) are the easiest to spot.   Of course, this
doesn't mean that each is like a flashing red light.

Extroverts(E) have introverted characteristics and
vice versa. After a recent presidential campaign someone
said of a particular candidate at a social event:
"Eventually, he will end up in a corner by himself."
Obviously, an **introvert**(I).   He could do all the
"extroverted" things: meeting people, talking, but within
he was constantly processing all the data.

Introverts(I) are "process" oriented. They constantly
view things, events, and future occurrences inwardly.
Introverts(I) have many conversations. Most of the time,
however, they are talking with themselves. A particularly
interesting way to recognize an **introvert**(I) is in their
slowness to respond to questioning. Usually the hesitation
has to do with their incessant need to "try and figure the
meaning behind the question." Few comments are taken at
face value. A max **introvert**(I) (meaning that the scores
on the <u>MBTI</u> are extremely high) manifests extreme
quietness and tends to be uncomfortable around others.

The **introvert**(I) is often misunderstood. He gathers
strength from within and usually makes decisions
independently of other sources. The **introvert**(I) is quiet,
works a great deal alone, and is often socially reserved.
An **introvert**(I) usually has to work a little harder to
remember names and faces. He likes to work alone and
hates interruption.

EXTROVERTS(E)

Talking, being fueled by others is the trademark of the **extrovert**(E). If an individual is a high **extrovert**(E), there's no doubt. He/she gets involved with people. Their orientation automatically involves others. While the **introvert**(I) gets dragged down from too much involvement and activity with others, the **extrovert**(E) is actually fueled by it.

I once tested a suite of ten senior college girls and followed their activities all year. All ten were high **extroverts**(E). Their suite was a constant beehive of activities: parties, people coming in and going out constantly. How they studied was beyond me. In fact, how they all graduated is miraculous.

Extroverts(E) may be the person talking to strangers on the bus, the elevator, or hanging out in bars. Once on a flight from Atlanta to D.C., I sat beside a seventy five-year-old **extrovert**(E). How do I know? She talked my ears off all the way. Even when I was reading or writing, she was talking. She told me about her four sons, her extensive travel, and subtly tried to emotionally hustle me (what a compliment)!

She was president of her Senior Citizen's group and was rushing back for the meeting because she's never missed one. Her group had one hundred and sixty four members, and she could count on one hundred and twenty five present at all meetings. Hustling them to travel over three continents was her joy in life.

I could fill a book on all the things she told me: seamstress, raised four children, husband sick for twelve years before he died, people helping her constantly. In her case, her extreme extroversion worked to her advantage. Most **extroverts**(E) have an enormous amount of energy. She sewed, kept her family moving, hustled her customers (she told me about several who always paid her double), and constantly had enough cloth (bought by her customers) to outfit her family: "Best dressed kids in Boston," she said.

High **extroverts(E)** are constantly thinking out loud. What comes from their mouth is a wonder to all. In fact, one max **extrovert(E)** confessed to me once that he was amazed at the things he said, "sometimes I hear myself saying something and even as the words are coming out, I'm thinking to myself, 'I can't believe I'm saying this.'"

POP PSYCHOLOGY
and
Introversion(I)/Extroversion(E)

I'm sure Jung never intended nor expected that his personality theory or part of it would ever be reduced to common usage. For instance, while watching a football game on TV, the color commentator said about one of the quarterbacks, "he is a shy and **introverted(I)** guy." What did he mean? He meant simply that the man was quiet, didn't like to be interviewed in the press, and preferred to remain in the background. The announcer captured it all by saying **introverted(I)**. Would Jung be pleased? I think so.

Still, we must be careful less we adopt the popular usage and lose meaning. For instance, I recently, gave the MBTI to a college professor friend of mine who tested out a strong **introvert(I)**. At first, he was chagrined that he could be an **introvert(I),** thinking like much of the American population: **introversion(I)** is not a desirable quality.

The more we talked, the more he began to see that he was indeed an **introvert**(I) and it did not have the negative connotations that he had been led to believe. It is not negative or positive, **it just is!** Being an expert in a well known historical field, he could sit for hours and pour over old papers and manuscripts. In fact, he once spent six weeks, 7 days a week, 10 hours a day, studying old records in the British Archives. By his own admission, he loved it. Only an **introvert**(I) could have been content among the dusty records of the Archives. Working six weeks in the British Archives would probably drive an extrovert bananas.

CHAPTER VI

Practical Or Head In The Clouds

N ow you will:

♣   See precisely how you look at life or your perception
     of things.

♣   Discover whether you are a practical, reality type or a
     projects and possibilities person.

♣   Nail down exactly how you see the data as it comes at
     you.

Sensing(S) and Intuition(N)

Looking at life through the eyes of an **intuitive(N)** or
sensing(S) type is akin to a parachute jump. The
sensing(S) type is involved in the mechanics of how it all
comes together: the chute fits, how it is hooked up, what
will happen when it is time to jump, who will give the
orders to go, what will happen when they hit the ground,
who is in charge. On the other hand, the **intuitive(N)**
person feels the wind in their face. The adrenalin is
pumping, the imagination of the experience is about to take
place, little thought is given to the why, only that it is about
to happen. Jung calls it "object" oriented. What I think he
means is the influence of the end result.
    The two terms are also Jungian to the core. However,
they have not enjoyed the public use of **introversion(I)**
and **extroversion(E)**. How people see facts or data
coming at them depends upon whether they are **sensing(S)**

or **iNtuitive**(N) types. It is the perception of the data, the happening, the event.   A **sensing**(S) person and an **iNtuitive**(N) person will not see the same data alike. **Sensing**(S) types are hands-on persons. They like facts. A good friend uses the example of two people standing on a pier watching a boat coming through the mist.   The **iNtuitive**(N) type says, "Here comes the boat."   The **sensing**(S) person says, "Yes, but it's not here yet."

I am constantly amazed at a friend who can hover over a desk for eight hours and never even flinch. He would search for days to find a missing penny in his checkbook and enjoy the process. One of my colleagues counted that I got up from my desk twenty eight times in a two hour period. If my checkbook is within a few dollars, I think it's great! Then again, **iNtuitives**(N) think that way. The **sensing**(S) person is the "salt of the earth."   Great at following directions. Simply stated, if you want to get a job done, get a **sensing**(S) type to do it . If you want to figure out a better way to do a job, find an **iNtuitive**(N).

iNtuitives(N) respond to the "what ifs" or "maybes" of life. They are   projects and possibilities people. They are the "heads in the clouds, the romantics of life."

Sensing (S) types are detail oriented, factual, trust things they can reach out and touch. They respond to the senses: see, feel, smell, touch. Attention to detail, two follows one, and B comes after A. This is order and order equals understanding.

The **iNtuitive** (N) type sees the possibilities in everything. He always has a better idea; "Dear, why don't we go to a movie tonight and then out to eat."   The **iNtuitive**(N) person will suggest maybe a play, floor show, eating before or after, or it may be time to go on a diet.

Robert Ludlum, in writing all the intricate spy thrillers where the reader needs a calculator and computer with a memory to keep up with the characters is an **iNtuitive**(N) mind. You can bet on it.

I still remember a Lieutenant when I was in the Army. He was leaving the service in a month and didn't have a great deal to do. Therefore, he decided to read Doctor Zhivago. Walking into his office, was like going into a war room. He had one complete wall plastered with the names of characters while the other was filled with the different plots. The author of Zhivago was surely a high "N".

The **sensing**(S) person is the practical one. He isn't staring off into space, thinking he is "Miniver Cheevy," he deals with the here and now. The **sensor**(S) looks at the facts, remembers details, is patient, careful, and systematic. If you want somebody to do a job, stick with it until it's done, be thorough, give attention to detail, give it to an "S". The **sensor**(S) is a master at following directions. However, if you want him to come up with a better way to do the job, forget it.

When people have trouble with "points of view," the problems are perceptual. **Sensing**(S) and **iNtuitives**(N) simply do not see the data in the same way. **Neither is wrong, just different**

Feeling(F) and Thinking(T)

Someone who values the meanings of life and how they relate to humankind is the **feeler**(F). The **feeler**(F) considers how his actions are going to make others feel. They see the beauty of the sunset and the blooming of the flowers. Great at smoothing ruffled feathers. The feeler(F) is moved when watching a sad movie, gets all teary eyed at the fond remembrance of the past. Watching a sunset, new fallen snow, leaves turning gold, would stir the feeler(F) to the toes. Other people are tremendously important to feeling(F) types, and their decisions reflect their relationships.

The thinker(T), on the other hand, is logical, analytical; he sits back and asks why, where, how. The thinker(T) is more prone to talk about "objective data." It doesn't mean that he/she has no "feeling," just that he/she has more of a tendency to come at it from the "head" first.

The feeling(F) type heads out to buy an automobile. He/she may start with the same logic of a thinking(T) type. They may have price, model, color, financing: all the questions in tidy order. However, suddenly they may find something they like and throw all the former decisions aside. Feelings for, about, because of something becomes the driving force in their lives.

Sensitive people who empathize with others are often found to be feelers(F). Emotions play a big part in their existence. Based on the degree of feeling, emotions for this individual can be the guiding principle of life itself.

I once had to interact with several churchmen over a period of months. Of the twenty three, twenty one were feeling(F) types. We constantly had to talk about each other's feelings about a particular matter (often when, to me, the issues didn't warrant the "feeling" scrutiny they received). In addition, the value ladened issues were never dealt with at face value, but always from an intensity that can only be produced when high feelers(F) gather.

Obviously, there is nothing wrong with this. It may not be as efficient as I, the thinker(T), would like. The truth of the matter probably is that their intense sensitivity and high level of **feeling**(F) probably brought them into their profession in the first place.

Thinking(T) types are "head oriented" people. They make decisions based on a rational analysis (they certainly don't call it such) and logic. If you ask a **thinker**(T) something, he will give you an answer to the question.

When in the process of trying to decide on an issue, the **thinker**(T) will come at it with a pronounced degree of logic. Going out to buy an automobile, a **thinking**(T) type, unlike the **feeler**(F), will decide on things like color, cost, availability, model. They'll check out Consumer's Guide, have a plan. **Thinking**(T) types do a great deal of asking "why, where, how, and when." They will usually do what they start out to do.

Feelers(F) are the opposites of **thinkers**(T); the great romantics of the world. Their decision-making processes are shrouded in mystery, more often than not rooted in the "gut."

Chapter VII

THINKING AND FEELING

Emphasis in this chapter is on:

 The decision making process

 Heart vs Head

I FEEL AND I THINK

Someone who values the meanings of life and how they relate to humankind is the **feeler**(F). The **feeler**(F) considers how his actions are going to make others feel. They see the beauty of the sunset and the blooming of the flowers. Great at smoothing ruffled feathers. The **Feeler**(F) is moved when watching a sad movie, gets all teary eyed at the fond remembrance of the past. Watching a sunset, new fallen snow, leaves turning gold, would stir the **feeler**(F) to the toes. Other people are tremendously important to **feeling**(F) types, and their decisions reflect their relationships.

The **thinker**(T), on the other hand, is logical, analytical: sits back and asks why, where, how. The **thinker**(T) is more prone to talk about "objective data." It doesn't mean that he/she has no "feeling," just that he/she has more of a tendency to come at it from the "head" first.

The **feeling**(F) type heads out to buy an automobile. He/she may start with the same logic of a **thinking**(T) type. They may have price, model, color, financing: all the questions in tidy order. However, suddenly they may find something they like and throw all the former decisions aside. Feelings for, about, because of, something becomes the driving force in their lives.

Sensitive people who empathize with others are often found to be **feelers(F)**. Emotions play a big part in their existence. Based on the degree of feeling, emotions for this individual can be the guiding principle of life itself.

I once had to interact with several clergy over a period of months. Of the twenty three, twenty one were **feeling(F)** types. We constantly had to talk about each other's feelings about a particular matter (often when, to me, the issues didn't warrant the "feeling" scrutiny they received). In addition, the value ladened issues were never dealt with at face value, but always from an intensity that can only be produced when high **feelers(F)** gather.

Obviously, there is nothing wrong with this. It may not be as efficient as I, the **thinker(T)**, would like. The truth of the matter probably is that their intense sensitivity and high level of **feeling(F)** probably brought them into their profession in the first place.

Thinking(T) types are "head oriented" people. They make decisions based on a rational analysis (they certainly don't call it such) and logic. If you ask a **thinker(T)** something, he will give you an answer to the question.

When in the process of trying to decide on an issue, the **thinker(T)** will come at it with a pronounced degree of logic. Going out to buy an automobile, a **thinking(T)** type, unlike the **feeler(F)**, will decide on things like color, cost, availability, model. They'll check out Consumer's Guide, have a plan. **Thinking(T)** types do a great deal of asking, "why, where, when, and how." They will usually do what they start out to do.

Feelers(F) are the opposites of **thinkers(T)**: the great romantics of the world. Their decision-making processes are shrouded in mystery, more often than not rooted in the "guts."

Chapter VIII

LIVING OUT YOUR LIFE

Y ou will see, in this final overview of the individual factors that make up the whole:

🜊 Your lifestyle or how you live out your life.

🜊 The degree to which you come to closure or your open ended attitude, always looking for more information.

🜊 The way to recognize the **judging**(J) or the **perceptive**(P) factor in your own life.

Judging and Perception

The **J-P** line is the final equation of the individual **Personality Factor.** Of all the **factors,** this one for me has the most utility. As an ardent "type watcher," checking out the **J-P** characteristic can be extremely useful. Isabel Myers, based on her mother's research, and observation added this concept to her theory. Ms. Myers saw the **J-P** line as important because it identified the dominant process. **J,** meaning **judging,** does not mean judgement as P, meaning **perceptive,** does not connote greater understanding.

As a theorist, her observations are right on the mark. However, for me, from extensive counseling situations, I have found the utility of knowing and pointing out the dominant process less useful than counselees' understanding the significances of differences and likenesses. **J-P** are the lifestyle lines. People live out their lives either as a **Judging**(J) or a **Perceptive**(P) person.

The **judging**(J) person has a pretty good idea of how he/she wants to live life and how others **should** live theirs. The **Judger** (J) is organized, likes orderliness, can tell you today where he/she will be next week at the same time. The **Judging**(J) **type** person likes control of the situation, can make a decision on the spot, and stays with something once begun.

The **perceptive**(P) type is open to changes, always looking at options. He/she is flexible toward change, open ended, appears unorganized. He/she has no need to control, preferring to compromise. Looking at all sides is a strong trait. The **P type** is always looking for more information.

Of all the factors, this one finds its significance in the observable here and now more than the others. I can only guess that you are an **extrovert**(E) or **introvert**(I), but I can see the way you live. The disorderly desk, the unbalanced checkbook, lack of schedule, most likely will mean you are a **Perceptive**(P) **type.**

The strictly keeping of a schedule, complete with one or more appointment books more than likely indicates the **J type** personality. I have a friend who carries a small pocket calendar with him. He has a large one on his desk, and his secretary has an identical one with his schedule as does his wife. Now, you tell me what his personality is!

What Does It All Mean

Perceptive (P) **types** start from point A going to point B and along the way, if they get a better offer, they are likely to take it. **Perceptives** (P) are often unbelievably open ended. They get accused of being indecisive when, in actuality, they are merely looking for more information.

Judging(J) types are organized, make decisions, keep commitments, and can tell you today what they're going to be doing next week this time. They are organized people, keep calendars, and know the direction they're moving. Efficiency is the order of their day.

Just as the **judging(J)** types are organized, the **perceptives(P)** are the "fly by the seat of the pants" individuals of the world. It is not that they are unorganized as much as they listen to the "beat of a different drummer."

Because **Js** and **Ps** are so readily observable, the trait is seen in children more easily. Adults learn how to mask their true feelings and perform what they consider to be correct behavior. In other words, they adapt quickly. *No value judgment, they simply do.* Children are prone to be just what they are. Add to this, their natural spontaneity and parent's inability to accept individual differences and you've got problems.

J type parents with **P type** children can experience much heartache. **P type** children come across as argumentative, often belligerent, and nonconformist. The exact opposite qualities that the parents want and desire, especially if they are themselves **J types.**

Chapter IX

TYPE WATCHING

The emphasis in this chapter is:

  Understanding the principles of combining **factors** creating the whole.

  Memorizing your **Personality Type** i.e. (**ENTP**) and its meaning.

Combination of the Factors

In math, a factor is any of two or more quantities which form a product when multiplied together. This fact is a key one to recognize. It is the combination that makes up the **personality.** For instance a **sensing(S)** person may be detail oriented and want exactness in life. When this is combined with **extroversion(E), feeling(F),** and **judging(J)** adding up to a combination of **ESFJ,** the overriding need is to please the significant people in his/her life. The person still wants exactness but the overriding characteristic will be the need to please.

The individual characteristic of desiring a factual and exact way of life loses out to the combination of "need to please." Consequently, we can conclude that the combination became the key in one's personality. A single factor may have significance but several add up to form the product (personality).

Two children are born into the same family, same stimuli, and yet they are vastly different. Why? They have different personalities. The <u>MBTI</u> measures those different personalities and lets you start dealing with your children based on their personalities and yours.

Many parents wring their hands convinced that because their children are not what they should be or what they observe in others, it is somehow their fault. What a revelation for them when they measure **Personality Type** with the <u>MBTI</u> and discover that behavior is more the result of the **Personality Factor** rather than parental influence.

You have a son who just can't seem to "get it together." Sixteen, argumentative, always going against what the rest of the family wants. In your estimation, he's hard-headed, selfish, thoughtless, unconcerned. Is it a stage of life or is he just a "bad kid?" More than likely, it's his **Personality Factor.** Certain **personality types** simply have a more difficult adolescence than others. Common sense combined with understanding the differences in the PF can make parental life much easier.

I remember talking to a mother who gave me the real life saga of her two daughters, ten months apart. One is the epitome of everything a mother could want: good student, excellent seamstress, cleans up her room, responsible in everything. The other has the opposite characteristics: no academic star, obstinate, irresponsible toward chores, a free spirit, often tuned into a different channel.

The mother had been told by a well-meaning counselor that the problems were because the second daughter was born so quickly after her sister. The mother's feelings of anger toward the husband for her pregnancies and the resultant hostility toward the newborn daughter naturally projected into the feelings of being unwanted for the child. Consequently, daughter number two is acting out and consequently, somehow, it's the mother's fault.

Freud's disciples and vast numbers of adherents to various theories, often have a field day with such situations. While some of her mother's feelings may have been projected to the daughter and she shows a lot of insight, more than likely, daughter number two's **personality type** makes her what she is. Daughter number two is, in fact, a neat kid, just different.

When I talk to distressed parents, I go into great detail to explain that they might have a child who is different from what they'd like; that it's a matter of the **PF**, and they can live with the differences quite successfully. And yet, parents continue to march to the tune of unenlightened school systems, experts, and generally accepted, but untrue maxims that children can be shaped into what they should be. Not so, children can be guided if a parent recognizes early the principle of the **PF** and capitalizes on it.

Knowing your **type** helps you to understand yourself, your family, neighbors, working compatriots, sweetheart, competitors, public figures. This doesn't mean "pigeon holing," stereotyping or labeling. It simply is a process of accepting the **Personality Factor** and seeing the differences in people. Your observation is natural. There's no magic in being able to recognize a person's **type**. However, there is a distinct advantage in it. If you can recognize a person's **type**, then you have some sort of handle on your relationship.

A few years back, a buddy and I began a marriage and family therapy practice. After a few months, his comment was "you've got to get away from **typing** people, we can't make any money." What he meant was that in order to have a successful counseling practice, we needed to keep people coming back. Clients would come in, I would give them the **MBTI** and immediately reduce a dozen sessions to three with no need for the background history gathering that merely rehashed and opened old wounds.

The short personality profiles that follow are the results of seven years of work. I developed them through the counseling experience. Most of my clients have taken the <u>Myers Briggs Type Indicator.</u> As I worked with them in counseling, got to know their personalities, and they became more familier with the terminology of PF, I would literally write out their profile and ask them to carefully scrutinize the result. I would pitch out those things my clients said didn't fit and leave in those characteristics that did. Sometimes, there were items that seemed to be generally in common but occasionally clients said, "no, it doesn't fit." I would hold some items for a time. For example, **ENFPs** as a rule, all seem to like "rings". It was just a personal observation in watching my two daughters who happen to be **ENFPs**. Over the years I've noticed that male **ENFPs** seem to be less interested in jewelry. How valid is such an observation? I don't know, other than it just seemed to fit.

By now, thousands of people have read the profiles and I've asked the same questions. When I've gotten an item that after much questioning didn't fit, I've thrown it out, even after all those years. It is in keeping with my philosophy: **only the individual can say truly what his/her personality is!**

Read over your **Personality Factor**, see what fits and if something doesn't, no problem. Remember, **only you can decide.**

ESFJ (Hard Charger)

You are the epitome of cooperation. Your desire to please overrides almost every other aspect of your existence, especially those who are significant to you. The very thought of someone not liking you can be demoralizing. You are the caretaker, sparing no effort to look after the well-being of family, friends, and the down-trodden. You feel good when you are sacrificing for others, and are hurt when your good works go unappreciated.

You like tradition, but you also like it to have meaning. There is a right way for things and people to be, and you like for that to take place. However, you will tolerate less than perfect in the "significant others" in your life. You respond to authority and to those who have position. *Your respect for the office can lead you into unwise decisions and to the extreme, even emotional and real disaster.*

Because you were an obedient and compliant child, you expect your own children to be the same way, and when they aren't you are bewildered and blame yourself. Your relationship with your children and your own feelings of self worth are often interwoven. **Be cautious less you read too much into every little happening.**

You are great at remembering special occasions but often expect payment in kind. This does not happen with great regularity. In addition to much disappointment, if you always expect something to come back to you, relationships can get to be very conditional.

You can do almost anything you choose as long as it involves people. You lean toward occupations that allow you to fulfill the needs of others: sales, the ministry, nursing, whatever, as long as you can be involved with others and do good. Your feelings of service extend all the way from the work areas to socializing.

You are a great host or hostess, never sparing an effort for your guests. *Your emotional well-being depends upon acceptance and approval.   This often causes you to try harder than is necessary.*

ENTP (Power Broker)

You are the classic possibilities and projects type. Ordinarily, you like to be with people. Most of the time, you are logical, figuring the pros and cons of most situations. You are always looking for new ways to do things. **Freedom is a big issue**: to be able to do your own thing and not conform to what others are doing. *You don't make a good follower unless you can see the logic in it.* Political parties and great causes don't excite you unless you see a reason for their existence.

You have a great gift in getting people excited about projects, but when it starts to roll, you lose interest and head off in search of a new challenge. *Boredom is an anathema to you.*

Your work probably expresses your nature more than anything else. If you are in a job that requires performance tasks with your hands, you often get frustrated. Thinking about the best way to do something and figuring out ways to do it are your strong assets.

Many jobs are open to you, especially if they are activity oriented. The routine task that involves repetition or mundane activity holds no interest. You would be intrigued with automotive engines or even how complicated machinery might work; but to involve you in the repair of one would be asking too much.

You do best where you are the boss or can even work alone: you call the shots, make the decisions, letting your success rise or fall on your own creative energies. In cases where you have to conform to a prescribed set of rules such as when you come to work, what you do, and when you go home is not to your liking. Writing your own job description would be your best bet.

You are a good manager of people, sizing up quickly how things and people operate. A field that might particularly appeal to you is teaching where you can devise new and exciting ways for the same old subjects. Counseling comes easy to you. In addition to good listening skills, you have a knack for getting to the heart of problems. The law might also appeal. It allows for your argumentative side which especially excites you. Whatever your choice, freedom is the key. Boredom then is manageable.

ENTJ (Power Broker)

You can take charge of any organization and run it. You are especially skillful with people, and they usually like you immediately. *Sometimes your people skills make you want to please too many people, and this becomes a burden rather than a blessing.*

Energetic and task oriented, you are able to do several jobs at once and do them well. People are often overwhelmed in your presence, wondering how you are able to accomplish so many different things.

Order is a big thing. Confusion in any area of your life is not easily tolerated: **a place for everything and everything in its place.**

Your life is in control and you feel that your "significant others" lives should also be in order. *Therefore, you pressure those close to you about getting themselves together.*

Logical to a fault, you want things to make sense and work. Consequently, you are usually good with organizing others because you are so together yourself.

Finances, for instance, are handled well because **security** is a big issue. You don't take too many chances. Risks fly in the face of your natural liking for order.

Careers for you could go in any direction. You are skillful at many things, and your organizational powers work so well for you, that no task overwhelms you. **The future is yours for the asking.** Your knack for organization, order, and control holds you constantly in good stead. The biggest problem may be getting into the kine aware of work where you can show your talent and be paid for doing it. You have a "take charge" drive which may get you into situations where you spend much energy without reward. This can become frustrating and may result in a series of career job changes.

When you're into this process, be extremely objective about what your chances are. If determined to "go for it," then keep searching until you find the organization wanting your talents and willing to pay for them.

You are first rate as a parent and homemaker. Your family means a great deal, and you are willing to make sacrifices for them if it doesn't fly in the face of your own plan. Because of your own needs, you occasionally have trouble with family priorities that may not fit into your scheme of things. However, your adaptability usually brings about harmony. You do best with a strong partner, who from time to time is willing to go head to head on issues, especially those having to do with child rearing. If your children go with your values, then the difficulties are reduced.

ENFP (People Catalyst)

You are absolutely captivating and charming. People are drawn to you like a magnet. Your vivaciousness and winsome ways endear you to most. You have a way of being able to get right to where individuals exist emotionally. You are sensitive to where people are and what's going on in their lives, especially how they relate to you. You are "felt" by those who know you.

You crave emotional experience. Friends mean much. You have many friends, but also want that very special one. When something significant happens to one of your friends, it is the same as happening to you. Perceptive, you don't waste any time going after what you want. *Many times you are **vulnerable** to relationships, tying yourself into people who don't or can't live up to your expectations. Learn to be more realistic.*

Life for you is like the curtain opening and closing on one great drama after another Everything interests you, especially if people and events are involved. Although jogging may not be a favorite pastime, to run in a road race that promises to be an "event" is something you'd do.

You look for the "real" in your activities. Loving spontaneity, you still want it to be **worthwhile** and have **meaning.** You inspire people and just your presence can turn a meeting, a social event, or gathering into something significant. **You detest the mundane,** but some routine maintenance things have to be done, i. e. paying the bills, servicing the auto, mowing the grass, cleaning the house. *Get into a habit of doing the mundane first and then get into those things/activities that excite.*

People get caught up in your activities. They look to you for guidance and answers. When projects are conceived, you are ready to jump right in, however, **follow-through** that requires your special attention can be an overwhelming task master. **Many projects may go uncompleted.** Beware less you take on too many things.

Your natural charisma will make you the leader when you really don't want to be. However, because you usually expect people to perform, they do. Skillful in not over-looking people's feelings, you go to great lengths to find a use for all talents.

Your choice of a life partner should be guarded, lest you find someone who doesn't know how to appreciate you. A good housekeeper or general "fix-it" person is not you, finding the tedious tasks of bed making, cooking or trimming hedges too much. Nice restaurants, catered parties, or gourmet meals are more to your liking. You love doing it, and even planning, but more as a participant or arranger as opposed to being a worker. However, you can do about anything that you set your head to do. Multi-talented. The possibilities of success are unlimited in any area unless the extraneous things of life overtake. Example: the extremely talented soprano who has the capacity to reach for the stars, but the high need for romance leads to a stifling marriage.

You are a good leader and immediately convey that you have something special to offer. There is no doubt that you are concerned and genuinely interested in those around you. You seem to have an inborn knack of getting in with the decision makers.

ENFJ (People Catalyst)

Most people like you immediately although you often have trouble concealing your **impatience.** Eyeball to eyeball communication is one of your best assets. You can communicate, and when people like you, they are caught up in what you are doing. You are especially good at seeing that which others don't see. The problem is that you expect them to have the same insights as you. This **frustrates.**

You don't mind getting involved in other's situations, and as a rule, you are good at suggesting ways for them to improve their lives. However, over identification creates problems for you thus making it difficult to extract yourself from the situation.

The **chameleon** effect is a real problem, and more than likely, it happens before you realize it. Understanding other's problems and realizing that in most cases there's nothing you can do is hard to differentiate for you. Keeping the situation in the proper perspective means that you have to stay **realistic,** not an easy task for you.

Organization is a plus and because of it, you often come across more knowledgeable than you really are, i.e. dazzling with charts and graphs, juggling the factual data. When people see the presentation, they are not above being overwhelmed with the material, even though your grasp of it is minimal.

You seek out perfection: at work, in relationships, and in organizations. This does not always happen, and when it doesn't, you may have trouble dealing with it. Frequent job changes may be a result of not finding the **perfect.**

Taken to the extreme, the same may be true of relationships; thinking that just around the corner is the perfect job, relationship, or situation. *Staying rooted in the "real world" must always be a priority.*

ESTJ (Hard Charger)

The best way to describe you is through your devotion to duty and responsibility. A good role model, bearing up under the load of responsibilities, your life is lived in a structured and orderly way. You operate best with factual data and information: "tell me the exact nature of the problem and what you need." If those are the directions, the mission will be accomplished. A plodder, not giving up until the job is done. Not easily discouraged. Never late for appointments. Task-oriented.

You are a great company person and can be counted on in any organization. You are consistent, honor the rules, and expect others to do the same. Loyal to the core. You do well in large organizations that appreciate and reward the time-honored "Calvinist" attitudes: hard work, punctuality, and sacrifice appeal. You would make an outstanding army officer or do well in a large corporation with a defined set of rules.

Because you work hard and accomplish much in areas that require "stick-to-itiveness," you expect others to do and be the same way; have your same ideals, be punctual, and observe all the rules. When this does not become the case, you have a tendency to become **intolerant** and **impatient,** and may even close off all points of view but your own. *Your "matter-of-fact" nature doesn't move toward people who operate in less well defined areas, especially those who talk a great deal about feelings.*

The same way you relate to institutions is the same way you approach relationships. Routines that have a purpose tend to spill over into your relations. Meeting your date on time, taking her or him to a nice restaurant, following the protocol and etiquette that bespeaks of the "right" way to do things is you. You remember birthdays, special occasions and holidays that traditionally have meaning. Straight forward. No double talk from you. *Learning how to plan and not take everything so serious may be a goal.*

ESFP (Fast Track)

You are warm and generous and go to great trouble for your friends. Your "significant others" are extremely important, and you sacrifice to the max for their well-being, even to the detriment of yourself. Your friends love you because you have a quality found in few people: making everybody welcome and glad to be where you are. You expend much energy planning your time to include other people. You are the consummate party-giver and goer. When people discover your presence, they know a happening will take place.

People and experiences are "where it's at" for you. You always make time for everybody. Much of your life revolves around trying to make sure that it all falls into place. You make people feel good and excited about life. Motivated, you often **flirt with disaster**. You work hard and play hard, and it's often difficult to tell which is which. A perpetual "Pollyanna" who can be expected to always look at the bright side.

Though your friends are quick to say you are great, they often don't take you **seriously**. Some may call you "scatterbrain." Becoming dissatisfied in your work and jumping from one thing to another is always a temptation, knowing in your heart that around the corner is just your thing. Your good **common sense** may give way to **impulsiveness** just to please. You hate hassle, and **peace at any price may rule you.**

You are an outstanding **salesperson** who has the knack for promoting products and ideas. Being around people that allow you to show your best results in high sales volume. You don't get rattled easily, and often do your best work in the midst of chaos. Always a cool head unless something goes against your basic desire to "enjoy." Your "eat, drink, and be merry" philosophy takes priority over most everything else. You could easily have been a flower child of the sixties. **Think about it!**

ESTP (Fast Track)

You are an action machine, never dull, things happening. You add a flourish to life seldom seen in others. A great sense of timing for the dramatic, you make the most routine affair seem important. You have a tendency to transfer action into relationships at work and play. Constantly in motion, you sometimes appear agitated even though relaxed. You are fueled by constantly living on the "edge of adventure."

You are an excellent communicator, specializing in getting to the heart of a matter. You don't hesitate to use this to your advantage, sometimes playing **oneupmanship.** Being in an environment where getting noticed is important, you have a knack for bringing it about. Pulling off the dramatic gets the attention of the boss by giving him exactly what he wants. Expediency is your thing. Even though your actions may grate on others, it is of little concern to you. You accomplish the end result because you grasp what is wanted. However, along the way your "end justifies the means" philosophy causes "bodies" to be strewn in the pathway. **Details** are not your long suit, others must take care of them for you. In most cases, the final product will be worth it.

A task must keep your interest. Your entrepreneurial skills are many. A salesperson supreme, combined with your winsome ways, causes people to tolerate you even as you flout the rules. Bosses who normally might fire or discipline workers violating company policies have a tendency to "accept you the way you are." Even with the significant people in your life, the **moment** is the important thing: eat, drink and be merry for tomorrow you might die is always your motto. If a friend or spouse can handle such a nature, life can be good and exciting; but if not, **disaster** can just as well be the case.

INFJ (People Catalyst)

You have an unusual depth in being able to feel deeply and make decisions about your feelings. You know exactly what you believe and have a real desire to translate those desires into action. You want to contribute to mankind above all else. Complex yourself, you search for personal insight and also have a rare capacity to understand the complexities of others.

You are an achiever who works hard and knows how to get what you want. Your perfectionist attitude causes you to put the very max into every task. Occasionally in school you are the over achiever. All things being equal, your natural ability may not add up to others, and yet your drive carries you over the top almost every time.

Often thought to be distant, quite the opposite is true. Your complexity makes friends who have known you for a long time see a mysterious side to you. Your **high need to please** makes hassle debilitating. You often scare people with your insight which borders on the extra-sensory. Both friends and acquaintances sometimes see you as **strange.** This is due to the keen inner vision which just as easily expresses itself outwardly in the realm of the future.

Writing or composing music or poetry is a strong pull because of your aesthetic nature. The poet in you is understood but more often than not, oblivious to others. One on one relationships are your choice. Crowds take too much energy and deplete your resources. Bringing to the stage a play that has depth, penetration of feeling, insight, and most of all originality is something you can do. Knowing and accepting yourself is important for accomplishing all you want. **Let it happen.**

INFP(People Catalyst)

You are a caring, sensitive individual who feels deeply about those around you.   However, expressing your feelings is not always so easy. **Causes** can come to have special meaning in your life, and you are not above giving yourself totally to them.

An inner sense of values drives you to make certain decisions, sometimes very much misunderstood by most. Occasionally, the logical wherewithal seems to elude you, and the tendency to take license with truth is more real than imagined. *However, you don't see it as such and are shocked when someone points out the obvious contradiction.*

At times, friends may accuse you of not being "present" with them. The absence is psychological, usually having to do with an inner processing, sometimes not even known to you.

You will stick with most causes or people for long periods, if a purpose is derived, that will help you in your caring concern for those around you. *You are short on understanding why others do not hear the same calls for the common causes as yourself.*

Being "all things to all people" is a constant attempt although not a conscious goal. Being able to relate to the group is far easier for you, as a rule, than to the individual. The individual relationship has to be perfect, and if there's the slightest hint that it is not, you feel somewhat that it is your **fault.**

You are adaptable and don't mind making sacrifices and even changing for the common good. However, there are certain intrinsic values that go even beyond relationships, and you will not violate those. Life is meant to have certain "shoulds" and "should nots" and without those there would be chaos. Most of the time, only you seem to know what those particular "shoulds" and "should nots" are.

ISTJ (Hard Charger)

You are the epitome of dependability. When there's a job to be done, you are the one to do it. You are a person of your word and could easily conclude a multimillion dollar deal by a handshake as well as a legal contract. You don't need stroking or pats on the back to accomplish the mission. You are the dedicated.

Work for you holds a special interest. Sitting before a computer terminal for indeterminate lengths of time, designing programs, or putting personal finances in order is your thing. Before making a purchase, you spend hours researching, listing the pros and cons. **Patient,** your philosophy is that if you stay with it long enough, eventually you'll be rewarded for your faithfulness. You are a good manager because you get the job done. *However, the people in an organization who don't share your strong desires for tenacity in doing the job can find themselves isolated and cut off from you.*

You **relate** to others as you do in everything else, : practically, preferring a few friends rather than many. You are loyal and trusted and can be counted upon. Faithful to the institution of marriage but in a stilted way, expecting it to be orderly and function smoothly. You are a great family member as long as all know and follow the rules with consistency. *You are hard on nonconformist members of your family as well as working colleagues who don't get the job done.*

Be especially sensitive to "feedback" about a sometimes intransient "no slack" nature. You may be bringing pain to the "special people" in your life, when doing such is the last thing you want.

ISFP (Fast Track)

You are a **now** person, choosing the present as your great motivator in life. Uninterested in history, especially the way things have been done in the past. You are **action** oriented. Let it happen is an unspoken motto. Usually energetic about those things which interest you: the call of the wild, sail the high seas, and climb the highest mountains translates your desires into action. **To dare for you is to do.**

You're the **craftsperson.** There are few things beyond you if you set your mind to it; the artist, the sculptor, the seamstress. You are sitting on "go" for your interests.

Those who love you will do well to appreciate your devotion to **experience.** You do not rehearse, you **do.** "Flying by the seat of your pants" is a special talent, usually unnerving to others. As an artist, practice is really not practice; everything is the act. Even your friends are baffled by your **unconventional** approach to life.

You make a concerted effort to **help** and never to **hurt.** There are almost no limits when trying to be of service, even to the exclusion of your own needs. You can be empathetic toward even the most undeserving and will occasionally continue to hang with a person who takes advantage of you, regardless of what others say.

Verbal communication is not your long suit although you have a strong capacity for understanding. You appear to be reticent to many, even shy. This coupled with your desire to be of service works against you personally, opening the door for many hurts. However, those who fail to look beyond the surface are the losers in the long run. You have much to offer a relationship.

When you truly throw your **energies** into something, you have a greater ability than most to stick to it, while at the same time, ignoring everything around you.

ISFJ (Hard Charger)

You have a great need to be of service to mankind. Totally unselfish, seldomly thinking of yourself, but always others. This extends to families and significant people in your life, but is not limited only to them, but also to charitable causes. You get your strength from within, and even during those times when you are the brunt of injustice, seldom stand up for yourself. You are a task oriented person who prefers knowing the rules, and once you accept them you stand ready to march ahead.

You **relate** easily to people who have needs. Because of your desire to be of **service**, you go to great personal **sacrifices** for those viewed as worthy, operating best around people who hold your same **values**. Loud and self-seeking people turn you off. You like people to act their age, not put on airs, and live with a certain degree of decorum. People love to have you as a friend, acquaintance, and especially as a colleague. They know you are **dependable** to the max. When you are assigned a job, it will be completed.

When a child is fortunate enough to have you as a parent, they get the very best. You are **traditional** in your approach to the family and love to see the "old ways" as a part of the environment. When you have children who are rule followers and adopt traditional values, you truly enjoy them. When they ask too many whys, you don't understand why they can't accept what is.

Your **dependable** qualities extend to your family. You love the well honored traditions of life, and you desire them for your family. Your homemaking reaches into all areas. You want a well-ordered environment, a home that is physically well kept and neat, a place that generally exemplifies your **view** of life. *You give **loyalty** and expect to receive it; and when you don't, you can feel rejected and even used.*

You want everybody to know the rules and accept them. Following a prescribed set of "the way things are done" comes natural, and you think all should feel the same. You work long and hard and are appreciative of all that you've accomplished, and you do not want it to be disturbed. Toward family members, this can often be translated as **inflexible, old fogey, stick in the mud,** and can cause rifts between family members if you aren't careful. Give some attention to your interactions, and don't be afraid to ask for feedback

INTP(Power Broker)

You usually appear quiet and reserved. Being logical is a strong point. When all around you seems chaotic, you can make **order** out of it. You are an idea person, someone who can take a seed and see the end result in your mind's eye.

Social amenities that are often forced upon you are a chore because you don't care to sit around and talk about things that seem to have little or no relevance.

You are a good, dependable worker, and as a rule put on a "good face" while doing the job. There are a variety of jobs in which you can excel. Because of the dominance of ideas, the mundane can be a stumbling block. Routine assignments which require little or no thinking don't excite you and avoidance is your usual out. *Employers who are tuned into the "nitty gritty" may see your avoidance as resistance, and at the extreme, laziness.*

You are **uninterested** in position or rank although you will be a good soldier and follow authority. However, you will not respect the authority if inconsistencies are revealed. If tasks are required but your principles violated, you can get very **stubborn**. If the taskmaster says it must be done, there is much gnashing of teeth, complaining and griping. You are interested in **practicality**. Getting to the point is a prime concern, and then going right to the heart of a matter or an issue. When understanding doesn't come to all involved, you are amazed because of your own understanding.

Teaching is to your liking, excelling especially in languages. However, even in those areas in which you're competent, you must avoid boredom. You are at your best when figuring out the best way to get the information across.

Writing your own job **description** which allows for accentuating strong points would be in your best interests. As an idea person, you need to be where those ideas can be put into practice. Working alone is no problem since you are a **self starter**. Making **decisions** without a great deal of extraneous emotion can be a great asset.

As a boss, you expect **excellence** and appreciate those who strive for it. You know how to be **firm** and can take **action** necessary to get people to respond. If they do not, you are not above firing them. Your personal **desire** to excel may cause people to feel you run over them roughshod. However, it merely has to do with your desire to get the job done and not to hurt others.

Analysis of the situation in any job is your long suit. Trouble shooting, for instance, is a good use of your talents. If there are supportive people around to implement your suggestions once you've diagnosed the problem, an organization will benefit greatly from your abilities.

You are the natural **translator** of theory into plans. You are great at telling people how to accomplish what they want to accomplish, but the **nuts** and **bolts** of getting the job done is another story. It's not that you can't do it, but you lose interest. **Once in your mind, you see the implementation, and have designed the bridge spanning the canal, others are left to build it.**

INTJ (Power Broker)

As an INTJ, you are a difficult person to **understand.** It is never anything intentional, rather a massive inner processing that may make you appear to be aloof, uninterested, or uncaring as to your surroundings. You are basically an unpretentious person and admire that same quality in others.

Your aesthetic side leads you into areas of gourmet cooking, stain glass, and various crafts that allow you solitude. Areas that interest you are given meticulous attention while others go lacking.

In relationships, you often appear unsure and hesitant, but inwardly you are generally devoted to a few **significant** people.

You have a **need** to do things yourself, and in an organization where it is necessary to **share** information, others are often left uninformed. Given the choice, you are a **loner,** but when you do interact you make it appear easy and relaxed.

Organization is one of your greatest assets. You put those things which have priority in the forefront. In seeking vocational choices, avenues where you can show your creativity and imagination will be best. Working solo in areas like **writing** or **editing** would be an excellent choice.

Your hard work often nets you more and more responsibility. You love **challenges** and will spare no effort to work toward solutions. Be careful that others are not trampled in the process. You are a **head** person as opposed to the **heart** and *if there's any area that you should stay attuned to,* **human relationships are it.**

ISTP (Fast Track)

You are extremely **introspective**, sitting back and checking things and people out before making a commitment. You don't hold back in doing your own thing, even if it calls for great risk. You have a keen insight into **translating** concrete realities into practical use. You are not above **flaunting** almost any rule. Impulsiveness is fueled by an insatiable desire to be where the **action** is.

You have a great talent for "hands on" activity, whether it be hang gliding or wind surfing. It's you against nature. You love to **grasp** tools: the scalpel, the wrench, the steering wheel. In the long run, this fascination leads you into **career decisions**. The illustrator, pad in hand, who loves to manipulate the stylus to transcribe on paper. You see your illustrations in everything and have the talent to get them on canvas.

For you, **planning** leisure would not make it fun. For play to reach the fullest enjoyment, it has to be **spontaneous**. You love to feel the wind in your face; riding the motorcycle, skiing, and being around other action oriented people. Sometimes, you don't participate, but always find pleasure in the activity of the other "crazies."

You don't see the **relevance** of talking just to be saying something or even to be **social.** You had much rather communicate your feelings by action, expecting others to see that what you've done speaks for itself. You can be **stubborn** and even recalcitrant in your views, "if there's no sense to it, I'm not going to do it." You are a "here and now" individual, and those around you who want to deal in the philosophical and theoretical don't do well with you. You are often **misunderstood.**don't let it get you down. In these areas where you can improve, and feel good about it, do so, if it gets to be too big of a hassle, **move to San Francisco!**

Chapter X

TYPE WATCHING

Focus in this chapter will center on:

☥ The practicality of looking at the world through **Personality Factor** eyes.

☥ The four corresponding Hippocratic styles.

Twelve years ago, when I began my passion for pursuing the **Personality Factor**, I had trouble dealing with all sixteen **types**. They were unwieldy and hard to get a handle on. Having been involved through the years in studying Hippocrates, there seemed to be some credibility to his observable behavior view. However, temperament implies moodiness and the **Personality Factor** is more in line with a fixed view. Call it fate, God, or whatever, but your **PF** is identifiable and does not change like the seasons.

STYLES

All of us have our peculiar "styles," that which sets us apart from others. This is, as I've said repeatedly, our **Personality Factor.** In over twelve years of testing thousands of people with the **MBTI** from every walk of life, I have identified four "personality styles" roughly corresponding to Hippocrates' *sanguine, choleric, melancholy,* and *phlegmatic.*

A **Hard Charger** *(melancholy)* is the person who believes in tradition, follows rules, and sees a prescribed way of doing things.

The **Power Broker** *(phlegmatic)* type is innovative and resourceful, especially good at motivating others. Loves challenges.

A **People Catalyst** *(choleric)* thrives on involvement with those around him. Sees service to mankind and people feeling good as life goals.

The **Fast Track** *(sanguine)* individual sees risk in terms of challenge. He or she can turn on to specific projects at the exclusion of all else. Is especially good at pulling things and people together.

THREE TYPE WATCHING EXAMPLES

CHILDREN

Two children are born into the same family, same stimuli, and yet they are vastly different. Why? They have different personalities. Recognizing the **Personality Factor** lets you start dealing with your children based on their personalities and yours.

Many parents wring their hands convinced that because their children are not what they should be or what they observe in others, it is somehow their fault. What a revelation for them, when they discover as they measure the **Personality Factor** with the <u>MBTI</u> that behavior is more the result of *individual difference* rather than parental influence.

You have a son who just can't seem to "get it together." Sixteen, argumentative, always going against what the rest of the family wants. In your estimation, he's hard-headed, selfish, thoughtless, unconcerned. Is it a stage of life or is he just a "bad kid?" More than likely, it's his **Personality Factor.** Certain **personality types** (People Catalysts, Power Broker) simply have a more difficult adolescence than others (Hard Chardgers, Fast Track). Common sense combined with understanding the differences in the **PF** can make parental life much easier.

I remember talking to a mother who gave me the real life saga of her two daughters, ten months apart. One is the epitome of everything a mother could want: good student, excellent seamstress, cleans up room, responsible in everything, a very identafiable *Hard Charger.* The other has the opposite characteristics: no academic star, obstinate, irresponsible toward chores, a free spirit, often tuned into a different channel (*Fast Tract).*

The mother has been told by a well-meaning counselor that the problems are because the second daughter was born so quickly after her sister. The mother's feelings of anger toward the husband for her pregnancies and the resultant hostility toward the newborn daughter naturally projected into the feelings of being unwanted for the child. Consequently, daughter number two is acting out and somehow, it's the mother's fault.

Freud's disciples, and vast numbers of adherents of various theories, often have a field day with such situations. While some of her feelings may have been projected to the daughter, and the mother shows a lot of insight, more than likely, daughter number two's **Personality Factor** makes her what she is. Daughter number two is, in fact, a neat kid, just **different**.

When I talk to distressed parents, I go into great detail to explain that they might have a child who is different from what they'd like; that it's a matter of the **PF,** and they can live with the differences quite successfully. And yet, parents continue to march to the tune of unenlightened school systems, experts, and generally accepted, but untrue maxims that children can be shaped into what they should be. Not so; children can be guided if a parent recognizes early the principle of the **PF** and capitalizes on it.

Knowing your **PF** helps you to understand yourself, your family, neighbors, working compatriots, sweetheart, competitor, public figures. This doesn't mean "pigeon holing," stereotyping or labeling. It simply is a process of once accepting the **Personality Factor,** you see the differences in people. Your observation is natural. There's no magic in being able to recognize a person's **PF**. However, there is a distinct advantage in it. If I can recognize a person's **PF**, then I have some sort of handle on our relationship.

A few years back, a buddy and I began a marriage and family therapy practice. After a few months, his comment was "you've got to get away from **typing** people, we can't make any money." What he meant was that in order to have a successful counseling practice, we needed to keep people coming back. Clients would come in, I would give them the **MBTI** and immediately reduce a dozen sessions to three with no need for the background history gathering that merely rehashed and opened old wounds. I left the business.

A Business Example

In the business world, if I can reasonably identify a person's "style," decisions are less clothed in mystery. For instance, there is a predictable personality that can go into an almost impossible situation, see the vision and do what is necessary to get the job done. This can't be taught at Berkeley, Harvard, MIT. It is the **Personality Factor.**

Over the last several years, I've tested scores of business executives. I'm totally fascinated by how little emphasis is given to the **Personality Factory** in gigantic monetary decisions. Large companies literally "go under" because they end up with not so much the "wrong" **personality types** at the helm as not having the "right" ones. Investment, portfolios, personnel policies are, more or less, the results of personality, rather than well-conceived plans for success.

PF enabled an obscure automobile executive, Lee Iococcoa, to become a household word. Iococca , (**Power Broker**), seen on the covers of magazines, in TV interviews, writer of a best seller is viewed in a Chrysler TV commercial where he's strutting through one of his auto factories and says, "Quality, hard work, and commitment, the stuff America is made of. Our goal: to be the best, what else is there?" If a *Power Broker* type is anything, he's a visionary.

Had Iococca had a high need to control, keep himself covered, and avoid risk, he never could have done the near impossible with his auto company.

Contrast Iococca with another "auto" personality: John de Lorean. My suspicion is that de Lorean is a **Fast Track** type. This is the person who plays his hunches, flies by the seat of his pants, and can have an unusual knack for pulling people together for projects (talking people out of millions of dollars).

August A. Busch III *(Hard Charger)*, ruler of Anheuser Busch, when told that Miller Beer was mounting a massive challenge to take the number one spot is reported to have said, "Tell Miller to come along but to bring lots of money." The clue to the personality of a *Hard Charger* is stubbornness.

Take any successful corporation and if dissected, **PF** will emerge. *People Catalyst* type tycoon, Trammel Crow, whose company built San Francisco's Embarcadero and redeveloped New York's Times Square is one example.

The mark of a *People Catalyst* centers around feelings, sensitivity, and subjective values. Reputation means everything. When Trammel Crow had cash flow problems during the recession, money lenders carried him because of his reputation as trustworthy. He has, reportedly, sealed million dollar deals on a handshake.

LOVE IS NOT ENOUGH

Bill and Betty met through their loneliness at a social club. Both had lost a spouse years earlier and had only recently began to yearn for companionship. They immediately hit it off and within months were married. The first few weeks were OK but not spectacular. Betty later admitted that even before marriage she saw some chinks in Bill's armor, but he was so perfect and she so lonely. He was stubborn, thought he knew everything, and had more than a touch of chauvinism.   Bill, on the other hand, saw that his perfect Betty had a few flaws . She was somewhat extravagant, a little too "clinging" for his taste, and impractical.

What do you have in Bill and Betty? Two opposites! A **Hard Charger** married to a **People Catalyst**.   This would be somewhat akin to Jane Fonda married to George Patten.   Marriage counselors have known forever that "opposites" attract. **Why** is the universal question? My belief is that in some crazy way we are attracted to those qualities in people that we don't see in ourselves. What happens is that "opposites" get tired of negotiating. As couples, they can't decide on which movies, where to eat, how to invest their money, and certainly not how to raise their children. When it gets too tiresome; splitsville. **I personally am convinced that this is the very reason we have so many divorces.**

After long years of counseling thousands of couples, testing thousands, not to mention a twenty five year marriage myself, I have concluded that people should marry out of "likenesses" not "differences." This becomes such a valid reason for discovering the **PF**. Unfortunately, usually when a couple arrives on the scene to be married, there's not much talking them out of it. Not that I'd want to other than point out the "opposites" and try to convince them to be ready for the problems..

I'll never forget a couple so "opposite" that I dedicated myself to talking them out of what I considered a colossal mistake. Making next to no progress, the event which sealed the non-contract happened in my office. The couple, obviously (at least to me) much in love could agree on nothing. They began to discuss the actual wedding ceremony. They could not see eye to eye on the wording, the music, not even the time of day. The discussion degenerated into a shouting match. In this case, the **Power Broker** (female) made an actual decision that she was not ready to marry this person, a **People Catalyst.**

THE ALIKENESS SYNDROME

Probably nowhere does the universal American belief that we are "all alike" show up like it does in marriage. An example: I heard a well known author and expert on love and marriage and family communications some time ago. His speech was entertaining and lively but dealt mostly with how marriages, to be considered successful, working and lasting, **should** be. For about twenty minutes he told his audience we will "make it" if we can just learn to be more romantic. He even gave us suggestions, especially the men, who are usually the unromantics. The answer: flowers, candy, househusbandry.

Then he really "hooked" us. "You must learn to tell your spouse how you feel. When is the last time you told her you loved her? Tell her what you really want." (Not bad advice.)

As he talked, I glanced over the audience. At least half kept getting lower in their seats. This man was a convincing speaker. An expert. Obviously what he says is true. **No, not true for all.**

My suspicion is that we can be reasonably sure that he is a **People Catalyst.** What he says is true for him because of his **Personality Factor** but not the natural choice for all **types.** For at least half his listeners, he was missing the mark. The speaker pounded like a giant sledge hammer on the heads of many who were doing the best they possibly could.

Incidently, **People Catalysts** seem to write the majority of the self help books, the novels, and in general are the media buffs. Thank God for them, but beware. Remember**, we are not all alike.**

WHY SO MANY DIVORCES

Is love enough? Yes and no. It is important and part of the great mystery of intimacy for couples. But, learning why in terms of personality is the secret to "making it" in a relationship. Only when an individual learns why his **People Catalyst** personality clashes with his **Hard Charger** partner's personality can there be any hope for salvaging what on the surface is an impossible relationship.,

Almost every year, approximately 1,800,000 people end their marriages. I can assure you, the **Personality Factor** was involved in all of them. Had these people known the whys of their **PF**, many of the marriages could have been saved.

Example: John is an elementary school principal and his wife of ten years is a college English teacher. John is fastidious, precise in everything, has a woodworking shop, great fix-it person, and often had just as soon be by himself as with others. Maggie is an innovative, creative female, who sees possibilities in everything. She adores people and loves to be with friends. She plans her social life with meticulous care, while John is content to stay home and be with his "little family."

John and Maggie won't make it unless they get off "dead center" quickly and get their collective act together. Discovering how their individual **Personality Factor** causes John to be the way he is and why Maggie has an incessant need for activity is the first step. Adjustment and compromise are the keys. Giving John and Maggie old tired remedies, even though true, will not hack it.

BELIEVING IN MAGIC

Human nature makes us want to believe in magic. In marriage in particular, we operate with these unrealistic Hollywood romance views. Movies and television have sold us a bill of goods. It's wine, cheese and an open fireplace. One step removed from Camelot. It just ain't so! Such an unrealistic romantical approach is impossible to sustain over a long period, but the **People Catalysts** will never give in! Ideally none of us should, but unfortunately we have to contend with our **Personality Factor** which is a part of our very being.

DOING THE BEST WE CAN

I usually tell people that there are three things that have to be done if a marriage is to make it: they must love each other, work hard, and if there's a third party involved, the situation must be resolved. The emphasis is on the hard work. No choice about the third party. Anything or anybody extraneous to the relationship cannot be. The hard work is the **Why.** The **Why** is the **Personality Factor** and once it's identified, then working toward solutions becomes the process.

Difficult, but not impossible. Our whole existence is built on change. **Just because we are born with tendencies to be the way we are does not mean we cannot change.**

ESTABLISHING BLAME

So many couples spend an inordinate amount of time blaming each other. A problem occurs and the screaming and shouting deals with "whose fault is it?" Not what can we do about it. Once you've bought into the **Personality Factor,** you can move on..

Look at Phyllis (**Hard Charger**). She arrived at my office with divorce papers in hand. I asked her why she'd come if her mind was already made up.

"Is Jim (**Fast Track**) cruel?" I asked.
"No, he's just no good."
"I don't understand."
"He doesn't work."
"Why?"
"He's had three back operations."
"So he can't work?"
"Well, that's basically it, but he doesn't want to anyway."
"He just lies around all day?" I mused.
"No, he does things."
He did do things: washed the clothes, ironed, cooked, did the shopping, handyman superb. Great househusband!

Phyllis and Jim had no children, both had been married before, with children by their first marriage. However, they were older and for all practical purposes, left to themselves. Phyllis was a career civil servant with a good salary. Basically, they had an easy life. However, Phyllis as a **Hard Charger** had a traditional view of marriage and a tough time accepting Jim's not working. **Hard Charger** types have a tendency to "lock" into a view that is consistent with the acceptable norm. However, Phyllis and Jim did not have a traditional marriage. Jim was the best "fix it" man in the community, cultivated a huge garden, canned, froze vegetables. When Phyllis arrived home every day, a full course dinner greeted her. Literally, she didn't have to turn her hand.

So you ask, what's her problem? A good clinical marriage counselor could find lots of potential dilemmas: lack of communication, unexciting. Jim may be "passive aggressive." Rather than fight with Phyllis, he fixes things. His communication, at best, is surface. In all probability, Jim isn't capable of the imtimacy Phyllis wants. One of the characteristics of Phyllis, the **Hard Charger**, is that she is often "singular" in what she wants. In Jim's case, Phyllis's understanding that Jim is "myopic" might turn the situation around. If she reads the "pop psychology" books, looks for the ideal level of intimacy, she'll be disappointed. However, if she wants her marriage, she has to accept some things about Jim. At this point, what each can live with becomes paramount. This is why understanding your **PF** is so very important. **Hard Charger** Phyllis and **Fast Tract** Jim are not going to change. They can make changes/adjustments, but their basic natures will not. Therefore, if they understand what they are confronting, their chances are much improved. Fortunately, they did. After ten years, Phyllis still has her divorce papers but no divorce.

Stopping But Not The End

There comes a time when there's an ending. With the **Personality Factor**, I have a difficult time coming to the end. For me, even as a function of my **PF**, I'm hooked on the **Personaility Factor**, and consequently, there is no end.

For the last ten years, learning about the **Personality Factor** has been my passion. I've been watching people for years spend thousands of dollars on therapy. The horror stories that I could describe personally would fill books. There are dozens of psychiatrists, counselors, therapists, consultants of all sorts who make small fortunes yearly off a couple of dozen troubled people who are trying in their own way to get themselves together. This doesn't even take into account the scores of other people trekking from workshop to seminar trying to figure out why they do the things they do and if they can do something about it. This is not to put down the helping professionals. The majority are honest and responsible persons doing for their clients what they can.

If you are one of the 1,800,000 people who ended their marriages last year, your **Personality Factor** was involved. You can count on it. Had you been involved in discovering your **PF**, your marriage might have been saved or at least from my perspective, you could have ended it knowing that for both of you, you've probably made the right decision. Simply, from a **PF** standpoint, we more likely than not, marry the wrong person. Marriage counselors discovered a long time ago that for some crazy reason, opposites attract.

Example: John is an elementary school principal and his wife of ten years is a college English teacher. John is fastidious, precise in everything, has a woodworking shop, great fix-it person, and often had just as soon be by himself as with others. Maggie is an innovative, creative female, who sees possibilities in everything. She adores people and loves to be with friends. Her planning of her social life is with meticulous care while John is content to stay home and be with his "little family."

John and Maggie won't make it unless they get off "dead center" quickly and get their collective act together. Discovering their **Personality Factor** through the Myers Briggs Type Indicator can be the first step in saving their marriage. Adjustment and compromise are the key. They can see it through their **Personality Factor**. Giving John and Maggie old tired remedies, even though true, will not hack it.

I occasionally talk to a writer friend on the phone. She's a creative poet and can come up with verse about anything or anybody. She's married to "Nevil the Nerde" who has the creativity of a pregnant eel. What usually happens in a marriage when strong creativity clashes with practicality: splitsville. Hope can result if the poet and Nevil can come to appreciate each other's differences. Grasping the concept of the **Personality Factor** can start them toward understanding.

I want to give the capability of using this tool to more people. The Myers Briggs provides instant positive feedback and truly helps people. Someone jokingly said, the Myers Briggs Type Indicator is like a fortune cookie, it tells what is good about you but doesn't talk much about the negative. However, what the Myers Briggs doesn't say may be as important as what it does say. Some truth, but for whatever reasons, professionals have kept the concept of the **Personality Factor** "light" under a bushel. I'm not going to speculate on their motives, other than to say that the hue and cry that psychometric instruments such as the <u>Myers Briggs Type Indicator</u> should not be allowed in unskilled hands is rediculous.

The **Personality Factor** is important to any large organization. I've tested hundreds of students, soldiers, business people. The institutions all have one thing in common: trying to fit all people into the same mold. If only they'd recognize the differences, their organizations would be appreciably better and productivity markedly increased, not to mention having happier employees.

The school system is the best example. Those blessed people called teachers who are overworked, underpaid, and underappreciated. To knock them sends shivers up my spine. Teachers are trained in a system which rewards good organization, promptness, neatness: all the "Boy Scout" qualities. Teachers love order. Discipline equals good education, and noise or disorder is bad.

However, children are not always orderly, do what their teachers would like them to do, or conform to all the rules. Why? They are all different. Yet, the system squeezes them to conform. Most do conform but some are destroyed in the process.

People have a right to be happy. I can't stand to go in and out the same door twice. Understanding my **Personality Factor** helped me understand why I drive my wife, friends and fellow workers "up the perverbial wall" by being unorganized. In my head, I know exactly what my priorities are, but my desk looks like fourteen hurricanes came through. My **PF**, at least, helps me not spend an inordinate amount of time "beating up" on myself. My **PF** helps me at least keep it manageable. **It can do all of this for you too.**

Just as importantly, understanding your **PF** helps you turn weaknesses into strengths in dealing with those interpersonal relationships which are unproductive. I've come to **appreciate** the differences in other people and myself. So can you.

Businesses intrigue me. Large ones, small ones. How some of them make it is beyond me, especially the "giants." Not long ago, I read two books which have made quite a splash in the business world: <u>Megatrends</u> and <u>In Search of Excellence</u>. Without going into detail, the books convinced me, not by what they say, as by what I know: personal success in business is not so much dependent upon following a prescribed set of business axions as it is upon the personality of those who run the businesses. The examples of why this is true are inexhaustible. Although I have mentioned John de Lorean before, he is a case in point. Putting all his troubles aside, he was destined to see greener pastures, attempt new ventures and maybe even set himself up for disaster. His **PF** dictated it.

When you read about the great machinations of corporate takeover, think about the decision making process. I can assure you that decisions made are only secondarily what is good for the company or the stockholders rather mostly a matter of the Personality Factor of the leadership.

Over the last several years, the helping professions have adopted the view that any type of advice is a **no no**. Comments like "owning your own problem, take charge of yourself," and other drivel is thrown back at people. Reflection and clarification are the key words. Once I went to a friend to get some advice, he kept saying, "What do you think you ought to do?" Finally in desperation I said, "If I wanted to know what I thought, I wouldn't be here."

People want perscriptions. I don't want anybody to tell me what to do, but at least give me a few possibilities.

I never met Isabel Briggs Myers. My loss. Working over the years with the <u>Myers Briggs Type Indicator</u> and reading <u>Gifts Differing</u> have been an immense pleasure. Her truths gathered over years of experience leaped off the pages, but one thing was most assuredly Isabel: no prescriptions. In fact, there were times in reading her material and that of her disciples that I wanted to shout "I understand the description, but what about a prescription?"

I know the Jungian purists and a few <u>Myers Briggs Type Indicator </u>enthusiasts are not going to like what I have to say. And, I do personally believe, people ultimately have to work out their own solutions. However, a little friendly advice, based on the **PF** belief is not going to hurt. The person who reads a profile based on the personality profile of the <u>MBTI</u> has to say, "My profile fits." Once they've said "It fits," then the flip side of the coin has to be, "Here's what you can do with it."

My iNtuitive fantasy is that the discovery of your **Personality Factor** through the <u>Myers Briggs Type Indicator</u> will become your philosophy of life. If you learn to **champion** your **PF** and conquer those aspects of your personality that are unproductive to you, you can truly be "all you can be, go all the way, reach for the brass ring." **Go for it!**